The Best Pet for Me

Is a BIRD
a Good Pet for Me?

Caitie McAneney

PowerKiDS
press.

New York

Published in 2020 by The Rosen Publishing Group, Inc.
29 East 21st Street, New York, NY 10010

First Edition

Editor: Elizabeth Krajnik
Book Design: Rachel Rising

Library of Congress Cataloging-in-Publication Data

Names: McAneney, Caitie, author.
Title: Is a bird a good pet for me? / Caitie McAneney.
Description: New York : PowerKids Press, [2020] | Series: The best pet for me | Includes index.
Identifiers: LCCN 2018046815| ISBN 9781725300927 (paperback) | ISBN 9781725300941 (library bound) | ISBN 9781725300934 (6 pack)
Subjects: LCSH: Cage birds–Juvenile literature.
Classification: LCC SF461.35 .M387 2020 | DDC 636.6/8–dc23
LC record available at https://lccn.loc.gov/2018046815

Manufactured in the United States of America

CPSIA Compliance Information: Batch #CSPK19. For Further Information contact Rosen Publishing, New York, New York at 1-800-237-9932.

Contents

Bird Crazy! 4

Different Kinds of Birds 6

A Bird's Life 8

A Cozy Cage 10

Bird Health 12

Keeping a Routine 14

Playing with Your Pet 16

Noise, Nibbles, and Mess 18

The Value of a Pet 20

What You'll Need 22

Glossary. 23

Index. 24

Websites 24

Bird Crazy!

Do you want a pet? A pet can be a great addition to your family. Pets can teach you the value of being **responsible** for another living thing. They can help you learn a lot about nature and animals. They can be fun and comforting.

Some birds make great pets. They can play games and fly around, and some can even talk! Birds can also be hard to care for. They are often noisy and messy, and they need the right foods and activities to stay healthy. Read more about birds to see if a bird is the right pet for you!

Pet Report

According to the 2012 U.S. Pet Ownership & **Demographics** Sourcebook, about 3 percent of households in the United States own birds.

Birds can be brightly colored, chatty animals. A bird might be the perfect pet for you!

Different Kinds of Birds

A number of bird **species** make good pets. Some of the most popular and friendly birds are cockatiels, parakeets, cockatoos, and parrotlets.

Parakeets, also called budgies, are small and bright, and they have the ability to talk and learn tricks. These birds, and many other species, often show **affection** for their owners.

Cockatiels are also small birds that show affection. They are part of the cockatoo family. Other cockatoos are twice their size! Some people want a big bird, such as a macaw. Hyacinth macaws are huge blue birds that can measure up to 40 inches (102 cm) tall.

parrotlet

Pet Report

Parrotlets are the smallest birds in the parrot family.

Pet birds such as budgies might sit on their owner's shoulders or cuddle up in their hands.

A Bird's Life

The more you know about your bird, the better. Birds start their lives inside hard-shelled eggs. Adult birds sit on the eggs to keep them warm until it's time for them to hatch. Baby birds are unable to see, fly, or stay warm. After a few days, they start to grow feathers and **develop** eyesight. Soon, they'll learn to fly and leave the nest.

Different bird species have different life-spans. Smaller birds tend to live shorter lives than larger birds. Large hyacinth macaws can live up to 60 years! Small parakeets can live for around 10 years.

baby parrot

If you get a large bird, it's a lifetime **commitment**!

A Cozy Cage

A pet bird's cage is its home. With the right cage, your bird can live a healthy, happy life.

The most important thing to consider when buying a cage is its size. Just because you have a small bird doesn't mean it only needs a small cage. Birds should always have room to fly, play, and exercise. Flight cages, or aviaries, allow birds to fly around freely and safely. Some cages have a top that opens up to let birds out easily.

Make sure the bars on your bird's cage are metal and spaced closely enough together so the bird doesn't escape or get stuck.

Pet Report

Birds' beaks grow continuously and need to be trimmed. Many bird owners put a hard bone called a cuttlebone in their bird's cage for it to chew on and trim its beak.

You can add perches, mirrors, climbing ladders, and toys to your bird's cage to make sure your bird has the best life possible.

Bird Health

Like all pets, birds need water and the right food to live. You must keep fresh water in your bird's cage for it to drink and bathe in. You should change your bird's water at least once a day and whenever the water is dirty.

Birds always need food to eat. They like to eat seeds, **pellets**, fruit, and vegetables. You should check with your vet to see what the best diet is for your bird.

Healthy birds have shiny feathers and plenty of energy. They want to eat and move around. Sick birds usually don't eat or move much and may be found on the floor of their cage.

birdseed

Pet Report

Foods such as chocolate, avocados, onions, and dairy products can be deadly to birds! Look for a full list of toxic foods before you get a bird.

You should meet with a vet when you first get your bird. They can help you find the right food and cage for your bird and make sure your bird is healthy.

13

Keeping a Routine

Pet birds need a daily **routine** that gives them enough time to rest and play. Most birds need about eight to 10 hours of darkness for sleeping and 14 to 16 hours of light each day for play and exercise.

Natural light keeps birds healthy. They need vitamin D from the sun, just like we do! Sunlight may also make them behave better. You can buy a special light that acts like sunlight if you live in a place where the sun sets earlier in the evening. Birds kept in darkness for too long may behave poorly or become unhealthy.

Birds are light sleepers and need almost complete darkness and silence to sleep. It might be helpful to have a **designated** bird room for them to sleep in.

Playing with Your Pet

A bird can become one of your best friends. However, it takes a lot of time and commitment to build a relationship with a pet. Birds are naturally wild animals, and pet birds have to learn how to act around people. **Socializing** your animal means talking to it, picking it up, and playing with it.

Socializing your pet can come in the form of teaching it tricks or games. When you teach your bird, the bird looks to you as its leader. It begins to trust you. Make sure to look up directions and work with an adult while training and playing with your bird.

Pet Report

One of the first tricks you can teach your bird is "step up." The bird will learn how to step up onto your finger.

You should spend several hours a day with your bird. You can hang ropes or ladders in its cage or in your bird room for it to play on.

Noise, Nibbles, and Mess

Before you commit to getting a pet, it's a good idea to learn about its less appealing behaviors, or actions. Birds are one of the noisier animals people have as pets. They can squawk, repeat words over and over, sing, and even scream! If you prefer a quiet household, a bird probably isn't the best pet for you.

Many birds bite and chew things. They might destroy the things in their cage if they don't get enough attention. Some pluck at their own feathers when they're upset.

Birds often make a mess! You must be willing to clean up after them as many times as necessary.

Pet Report

Birds need toys and interaction to keep them from becoming bored and **destructive**.

Some birds are known to be very **vocal**. Many scream because they are bored, **stressed**, or **depressed**.

The Value of a Pet

When it comes to getting any pet, it's important to consider what they need. As their owner, you will need to provide for them to keep them healthy and safe. You may have saved up enough money to afford to buy your bird, but you also need money for its cage, food, toys, and vet bills. Your whole family should talk before you get a pet!

Despite the challenges of owning a bird, there are many benefits. Many birds are funny, bright, and smart. They love to interact with people and learn new things. Do you think a bird is a good fit for your home?

Birds can be great **companions** if you care for them correctly!

What You'll Need

Fee: $15 to more than $1,000 depending on the species

Birdcage: $60 to $1,000

Food (pellets and fresh produce and grains): More than $30 to start

Food and water dishes: $8 to $30 depending on style

Nest (small): $4 to $12

Birdbath: $8

Vet exam: $50 to $200

Two perches: $12 to $30

Total estimated cost for beginning supplies:
$187 to $2,310

Glossary

affection: A feeling of liking and caring for someone or something.

commitment: An agreement to do something.

companion: A person or animal you spend time with.

demographics: The qualities of a group of people.

depressed: Low in spirits or sad.

designate: To officially give someone or something a particular role or purpose.

destructive: Causing ruin.

develop: To grow and change.

pellet: A usually small, rounded piece of food.

responsible: Having the job or duty of dealing with or taking care of something or someone.

routine: A usual order and way of doing something.

socialize: To teach to behave in a way acceptable in society.

species: A group of plants or animals that are all the same kind.

stressed: Feeling very worried or anxious.

vocal: Speaking freely or loudly.

Index

A
activities, 4
affection, 6
aviaries, 10

B
baby birds, 8
beak, 10
bird room, 15, 17
budgies, 6, 7

C
cage, 10, 11, 12, 13,
    17, 18, 20, 22
cockatiels, 6
cockatoos, 6
cuttlebone, 10

E
eggs, 8
eyesight, 8

F
feathers, 8, 12, 18
food, 4, 12, 13, 20,
    22

G
games, 4, 16

H
hyacinth macaw,
    6, 8

L
light, 14

N
nest, 8, 22

P
parakeets, 6, 8
parrot, 6, 8
parrotlets, 6
pellets, 12, 22

R
routine, 14

S
seeds, 12
species, 6, 8, 22

T
toxic foods, 12
toys, 11, 18, 20
tricks, 6, 16

U
United States, 4

V
vegetables, 12
vet, 13, 20, 22
vitamin D, 14

W
water, 12, 22

Websites